Editor-in-Chief and Founder:
  Lyndon H. LaRouche, Jr.
Editorial Board: *Lyndon H. LaRouche, Jr. , Helga Zepp-LaRouche, Robert Ingraham, Tony Papert, Gerald Rose, Dennis Small, Jeffrey Steinberg, William Wertz*
Co-Editors: *Robert Ingraham, Tony Papert*
Managing Editor: *Nancy Spannaus*
Technology: *Marsha Freeman*
Books: *Katherine Notley*
Ebooks: *Richard Burden*
Graphics: *Alan Yue*
Photos: *Stuart Lewis*
Circulation Manager: *Stanley Ezrol*

INTELLIGENCE DIRECTORS
Counterintelligence: *Jeffrey Steinberg, Michele Steinberg*
Economics: *John Hoefle, Marcia Merry Baker, Paul Gallagher*
History: *Anton Chaitkin*
Ibero-America: *Dennis Small*
Russia and Eastern Europe: *Rachel Douglas*
United States: *Debra Freeman*

INTERNATIONAL BUREAUS
Bogotá: *Miriam Redondo*
Berlin: *Rainer Apel*
Copenhagen: *Tom Gillesberg*
Houston: *Harley Schlanger*
Lima: *Sara Madueño*
Melbourne: *Robert Barwick*
Mexico City: *Gerardo Castilleja Chávez*
New Delhi: *Ramtanu Maitra*
Paris: *Christine Bierre*
Stockholm: *Ulf Sandmark*
United Nations, N.Y.C.: *Leni Rubinstein*
Washington, D.C.: *William Jones*
Wiesbaden: *Göran Haglund*

ON THE WEB
e-mail: eirns@larouchepub.com
www.larouchepub.com
www.executiveintelligencereview.com
www.larouchepub.com/eiw
Webmaster: *John Sigerson*
Assistant Webmaster: *George Hollis*
Editor, Arabic-language edition: *Hussein Askary*

EIR (ISSN 0273-6314) *is published weekly
(50 issues), by EIR News Service, Inc.,
P.O. Box 17390, Washington, D.C. 20041-0390.
(703) 777-9451*

European Headquarters: E.I.R. GmbH, Postfach
Bahnstrasse 9a, D-65205, Wiesbaden, Germany
Tel: 49-611-73650
Homepage: http://www.eirna.com
e-mail: eirna@eirna.com
Director: Georg Neudecker

Montreal, Canada: 514-461-1557

Denmark: EIR - Danmark, Sankt Knuds Vej 11,
basement left, DK-1903 Frederiksberg, Denmark.
Tel.: +45 35 43 60 40, Fax: +45 35 43 87 57. e-mail:
eirdk@hotmail.com.

Mexico City: EIR, Sor Juana Inés de la Cruz 242-2
Col. Agricultura C.P. 11360
Delegación M. Hidalgo, México D.F.
Tel. (5525) 5318-2301
eirmexico@gmail.com

Canada Post Publication Sales Agreement
#40683579

Postmaster: Send all address changes to *EIR*, P.O.
Box 17390, Washington, D.C. 20041-0390.

Signed articles in *EIR* represent the views of the
authors, and not necessarily those of the Editorial
Board.

Is Japan Really Going To Do This?

EIR Contents

www.larouchepub.com Volume 43, Number 22, May 27, 2016

wikimedia

**Cover
This Week**

*"The Great Wave
Off Kanagawa,"
a color
woodblock by
Katsushika
Hokusai,
1829-32.*

I. Bold Motion in Asia

Is Japan Really Going To Do This?

by Michael Billington

May 21 (EIRNS)—New initiatives emerged in East Asia this month, largely through the efforts of Russian President Vladimir Putin, with consequences that have greatly damaged the ongoing Anglo-American war drive, while opening up the potential for the integration of all East Asia into a "zone of peace," defined by the economic development perspective of the New Silk Road and China's "One Road, One Belt" policy.

On May 6, Japanese Prime Minister Shinzo Abe held an extremely successful summit with Putin in Sochi on the Black Sea, despite intense pressure from the Obama White House to

kremlin.ru

Despite intense pressure from the Obama White House, Japanese Prime Minister Shinzo Abe (left) and Russian President Vladimir Putin (right) at their May 6 summit in Sochi, Russia, discussed proposed Japanese economic joint development projects in the Russian Far East, which have the potential to undermine the geopolitical drive for war being championed by Obama.

cancel the visit. Sources close to the negotiations have informed *EIR* that Abe and Putin agreed on a path towards solving the territorial dispute that has prevented the signing of a peace treaty to end World War II between Russia and Japan.

The two leaders also discussed a wide range of potential Japanese investments, mostly in the Russian Far East, in oil and gas production, energy generation, medical facilities, transportation, ports, and more. The launching of such extensive joint development will also have significant implications for the Korean Peninsula, because the potential for joint China-Japan-South Korea-Russia projects in the Russian Far East, involving skilled North Korean labor, is a necessary basis for re-

solving the other crisis spot left over from World War II.

Then, on May 19-20, President Putin hosted the summit of Russia and the Association of Southeast Asia Nations (ASEAN), also in Sochi. The title of the summit, "Towards Strategic Partnership for the Sake of the Common Good," is, in and of itself, a strategic statement of the utmost importance, and it makes clear that Russia's intention is not to turn ASEAN against the United States, but against *geopolitics* itself. Before the summit, the government leaders of nearly all of the ASEAN nations issued strong endorsements of Russia's crucial role in Asia, calling for expanding Russia's relatively low level of trade and investment in the region.

President Putin hosted the summit of Russia and the Association of the Southeast Asian Nations (ASEAN) on May 19-20 in Sochi, in a further move against geopolitics. It was entitled "Towards Strategic Partnership for the Sake of the Common Good."

U.S. President Barack Obama will be in Asia from May 21 to 28, visiting Vietnam and Japan. As a result of Putin's initiatives, this trip will now take place in an environment in which his carefully nurtured anti-China alliance is beginning to fracture and collapse. It was in October 2011 that his anti-China policy, which Obama dubbed his *Pivot to Asia*, was first announced by his sister-in-war Hillary Clinton, in an article in *Foreign Affairs*, the journal of the Council on Foreign Relations (CFR), entitled, "America's Pacific Century." Obama's approach is that of the British Empire—imperial geopolitics—based on the notion that nations function in the same manner as the Hobbesian view of individual men and women: *bellum omnium contra omnes*, "the war of all against all," or each against all. This bestial view of man is the bedrock of the imperial strategy of divide and conquer.

As a result of Vladimir Putin's flanking initiatives, Obama's intentions have been dealt a huge blow over these recent days. Russia, in conjunction with China's leaders, has moved decisively to defeat not only

Obama's war plans, but geopolitics itself. The ability to manipulate nations against each other depends on convincing those nations that the degraded imperial view of man and nations is true, that a nation's self-interest requires the forming of military and economic blocs to protect against stronger neighbors, that there is no such thing as the common aims of mankind.

China is seen as a threat to the Anglo-American imperial alliance precisely because the New Silk Road concept introduced by Chinese President Xi Jinping— together with the BRICS New Development Bank and the Asian Infrastructure Investment Bank (AIIB)—is based on a win-win concept of mutual development for all nations. This challenges Obama's "we make the rules" mentality, and his effort to encircle China with U.S. military bases and real or imagined U.S. allies ready to join in a U.S. war on China. This war policy depends on Japan as the core of the military alliance.

But Putin has now weighed in with a brilliant flanking operation in East Asia, just as he flanked Obama through Russia's intervention in Syria, which exposed Obama as the backer of the very terrorists he claimed to be fighting.

Putin-Abe Breakthrough and Imperial Reaction

At the May 6 Sochi summit, President Putin invited Prime Minister Abe to attend the second Eastern Economic Forum in Vladivostok on Sept. 2-3. Abe is expected to attend, and to hold a second summit with Putin. The forum will bring together international business and government representatives to discuss the economic potential of Russia's Far East and the Asia-Pacific region, and the investment opportunities.

Yury Trutnev, the Russian Deputy Prime Minister and Presidential Plenipotentiary Envoy to the Far Eastern Federal District, followed the Sochi summit with a visit to Tokyo this past week. At the same time, the Chief Executive Officer of the Far East and Baikal Region Development Fund, Alexei Chekunkov, announced, "The Far East Development Fund has updated its portfolio of promising projects. We are offering 29 projects worth a total of $16 billion to Japan's investors," according to TASS.

Putin and Abe also agreed that Putin will visit Japan before the end of the year, and will meet with Abe in Yamaguchi Prefecture, Abe's home region.

In a frantic response to this dramatic intervention by Putin, the trans-Atlantic establishment is warning that the West has lost sight of Russia's potential role in Asia, describing it as extremely dangerous. *Foreign Affairs* released an article May 17 warning of "an emerging geopolitical reality: no Western leader knows quite what to do about Russia as it wields its strategic influence across Eurasia.... Russia, declining as it might be, is yet a serious Eurasian power to be reckoned with. The West has essentially treated Russia as a rival European power, largely failing to manage its Eurasian challenges since 2014.... From Serbia to Afghanistan, Russia is using a combination of energy deals, arms supplies, and covert actions to solidify its stakes in Eurasia's arc of instability."

Authors Joshua Walker of the German Marshall Fund (and a former State Department officer) and Hidetoshi Azuma of the American Security Project protest in the article that not only is Putin threatening to destroy Washington's effort to get Japan's military on the side of the war against China and Russia, but he even has the gall to speak out on Obama's provocative operations in the South China Sea: "As Beijing's latest solicitation for Moscow's support for its South China Sea policies demonstrates, Russia is also emerging as a significant actor in Asian seas, the stability of which is crucial to European economies."

The CFR duo try to find some light in the matter by pathetically claiming that Abe is trying to bring the United States and Russia together, based on cooperation against "the rise of China, where Russian and Western interests are aligned."

Even here, Abe has taken an important step to *improve* the tense relations with China due to China's legitimate concern over Abe's effort to change the Japanese Constitution to allow Japan to join the United States in a war on China. In fact, however, there has been no decline in the extensive economic relations between the second and third largest economies in the world. China is Japan's largest trading partner, and Japan is China's second-largest. Japan is the largest investor in China, with direct investment of more than $100 billion as of 2014, or $30 billion more than the next largest source, the United States.

Now, Abe has appointed a new Ambassador to China, Yutaka Yokoi, who is a China expert with deep experience in China, and is fluent in Chinese. In his first press conference at the Japanese Embassy in Beijing on May 16, Yokoi said, "I will do my best to move the gears steadily forward. I want to boost mutual trust by communicating well with the Chinese side and cooperating on many common interests and challenges." *China Daily* wrote an editorial calling Yokoi "a precious asset for handling the tricky relations at such a sensitive juncture."

In discussions this week, Lyndon LaRouche pointed to the profound implications of these recent developments. He asked, Is Japan really going to do this? If so, he said, what is in prospect is the closest, trusted cooperation among Russia, India, China, and Japan in Asia, in the political, economic, and security dimensions, which will revolutionize Asia and the world.

Putin-ASEAN

While Japan is supposed to be the core of Obama's anti-China bloc in Asia, the Philippines and Vietnam are the two front-line states in his effort to pro-

kremlin.ru

Vietnam has maintained close relations with Russia over the last decades. Here, newly appointed Prime Minister Nguyen Xuan Phuc meets Putin in Moscow shortly before the ASEAN summit.

Ministry of Defense

The newly appointed Vietnamese Defense Minister, Ngo Xuan Lich, made Moscow his first foreign visit, from April 23 to 29.

voke a war over the South China Sea, where these two members of ASEAN have significant, conflicting territorial claims with China. The Philippines has been central to aggravating tensions, where outgoing President Noynoy Aquino has served as a willing tool of

Obama's drive to destroy China's leadership of a new global economic order based on win-win development. In particular, Aquino set in motion the extremely provocative and dangerous re-occupation of the island nation by the U.S. military.

But Vietnam has also been courted by Obama to join in the military confrontation with China and Russia. Obama will be dangling the potential of lifting the U.S. ban on arms sales to Vietnam, which has existed since the ringing defeat of the United States in Vietnam War of the 1960s and 1970s. The arms sales are intended to endear Vietnam to the U.S. military confrontation with China.

Vietnam has in fact been in conflict with China over conflicting sovereignty claims in the Paracel (Xisha) Islands in the South China Sea, including some minor military confrontations at sea. While Vietnam will welcome the dropping of the arms sale ban, it has had no trouble finding other sources of military supplies—it is the eighth largest arms importer in the world. Nor has Vietnam allowed relations with China to collapse, as in the Philippines.

Here again, Putin's initiatives with both Japan and ASEAN have thrown a huge monkey wrench into the Anglo-American war drive, as the potential for great economic development projects, including the participation of Japan, has redefined the dynamic and potential direction for the entire region.

Vietnam has continued to maintain close relations with Russia over the past decades, and newly appointed Prime Minister Nguyen Xuan Phuc traveled to Moscow before the summit for bilateral meetings with Putin and Prime Minister Dmitri Medvedev. The newly appointed

Defense Minister, Ngo Xuan Lich, made Moscow his first foreign visit from April 23 to 29.

At the same time, the Chinese Ambassador to Vietnam, Hong Xiaoyong, met with Defense Minister Ngo on May 19 in Hanoi, where the two sides agreed to further strengthen military cooperation. Defense Minister Ngo praised the "friendly neighborliness, comprehensive cooperation, long-term stability," while looking towards the future as "good neighbors, good friends, good comrades, and good partners."

Even the Philippines

The results of the May 9 presidential election in the Philippines has been a wake-up call for the western sponsors of the semi-colonized Philippine nation. Outgoing President Aquino ignored his own nation's constitutional ban on foreign bases on Philippine soil by opening up military bases to U.S. occupation. Aquino was also praised by his sponsors for the nation's supposedly great economic progress, with the highest rate of growth in ASEAN. The fact that that "growth" appears on the books purely as a result of financial speculation, helps to account for the fact that the poverty and hunger rates have increased under Aquino's rule, while foreign control of the economy has increased.

The result is that a political outsider, Rodrigo Duterte, the Mayor of Davao City on the impoverished southern island of Mindanao, swept the election against the chosen candidates from the elite who have largely ruled the nation on behalf of Wall Street since the U.S.-orchestrated coup against nationalist President Ferdinand Marcos in 1986. Duterte is a wild card—and a bit of a wild man—whose policies are unclear. However, among his many promises—which include such outrageous promises as to kill all the criminals and feed them to the fish in Manila Bay—are several serious ones, which threaten to sever Obama's control over the nation and potentially to stop Obama's intention to use the country as a base for war on China.

One of Duterte's first meetings was with China's Ambassador to the Philippines, Zhao Jianhua, on May 17. Duterte had said during the campaign that he wanted to cultivate friendly relations with China, and was open to direct talks over the issues in the South China Sea. "If

Office of the City Mayor, Davao City

Rodrigo Duterte (right) has been elected President of the Philippines, sweeping past the candidates chosen by the elites who have collaborated with Obama in war provocations against China. Duterte, who said during the campaign that he wanted to cultivate friendly relations with China, is shown here receiving a book on Chinese President Xi Jinping from Chinese Ambassador to the Philippines, Zhao Jianhua, May 16.

the ship of negotiations is in still waters and there is no wind to push the sail," he said, "I might just decide to talk bilaterally with China."

Following the meeting, Ambassador Zhao said that Duterte has expressed his willingness to improve and develop relations between China and the Philippines, and strengthen bilateral cooperation to benefit the peoples of the two countries.

This is sending fearful tremors through the war party in Washington. It has spent the past months preparing to use the expected ruling against China by the Permanent Court of Arbitration in the Hague, in a case brought by the Philippines over sovereign rights in the South China Sea, as justification for a major military confrontation with China.

But the question of real development, through win-win agreements among nations—rather than geopolitical confrontation and austerity under the collapsing economic financial system of New York and London—has led the Philippines, at least potentially, to choose progress over war. Duterte has called on China to invest in his country through its New Maritime Silk Road and the AIIB, for the development of railroads, ports, and other infrastructure, a process desperately needed in the Philippines. This is not only progress, but the end of imperial geopolitics.

India's Water Minister: Linking of Rivers Is 'Top Priority'

by Ramtanu Maitra

May 22—After years of leaders in New Delhi being unwilling to prod the state governments on the linking of rivers to transfer water from areas with surplus water in one state to water-deficient areas in another state, it seems the government of Prime Minister Narendra Modi has decided to take the bull by the horns and has given "top priority" status to rejuvenating the water-transfer plan lying virtually dormant for more than 40 years—a plan long supported by Lyndon and Helga La-Rouche. It is an understatement to say that the challenge is daunting.

In the midst of an extreme drought that has devastated large areas of farmland and put millions of Indians' lives at stake, India's Water Resources Minister, Uma Bharti, told the BBC, in an interview reported by BBC World Service's Navin Singh Khadka on May 16, that "interlinking of rivers is our prime agenda and we have got the people's support, and I am determined to do it on the fast track." "We are going ahead with five links now and the first one, the Ken-Betwa link [in Uttar Pradesh and Madhya Pradesh states, see **Figures 1 and 2**] is going to start any time now. And then we will have the Damanganga-Pinjal interlink" (see Figure 2), which will help resolve the Mumbai drinking water shortage, she added. She also claimed that transferring water, including from major rivers like the Brahmaputra and the Ganga (or Ganges), to drought-prone areas is now her government's top priority (see Figure 2).

Dr. Rao's Plan

India's plan to interlink its glacier and rain-fed Himalayan rivers (having a water surplus) to the Peninsular rivers emerged in 1972, when an eminent Indian engineer, Dr. K.L. Rao, who

served as minister in the Nehru, Shastri, and Indira Gandhi Cabinets, proposed linking up the water-surplus Ganga, a Himalayan river, to the water-short Cauvery River. The Cauvery (or Kaveri), a southern Indian river, originates in the Western Ghats, a mountain range parallel to the west coast, in Karnataka state and flows in the south-easterly direction for 475 miles through the states of Karnataka and Tamil Nadu across the Deccan Plateau, before emptying into the Bay of Bengal.

FIGURE 1

The Indian States

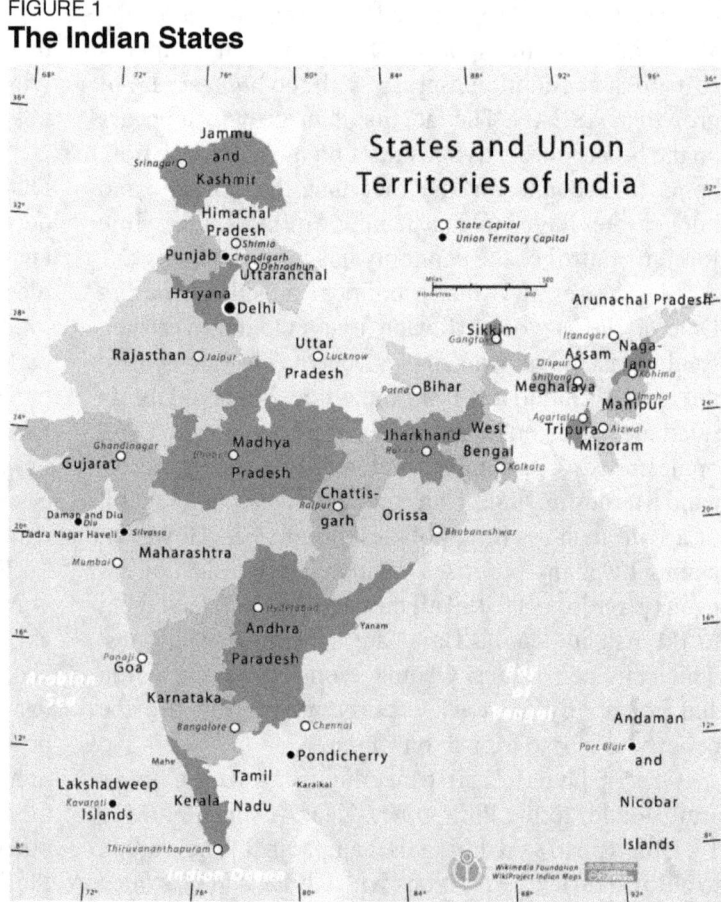

FIGURE 2
The Water Transfer Plan

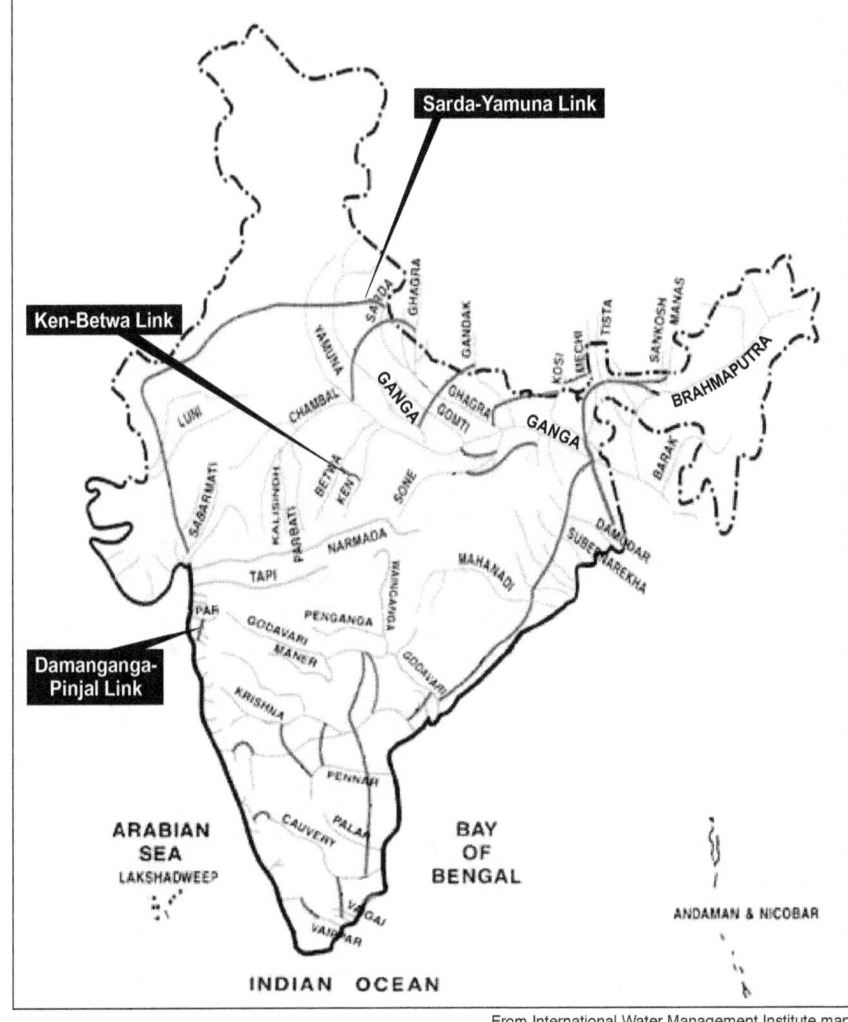

From International Water Management Institute map

The planned links between rivers are shown in red. The link from the Sarda to the Sabarmati is three projects—Sarda-Yamuna (shown in detail in Figure 3), Yamuna-Rajasthan, and Rajasthan-Sabarmati.

it would enable the irrigation of an additional 35 million hectares (ha)—about one-third of China's entire arable land—and the generation of 35 gigawatts of hydro-electric power, in addition to providing some navigation and flood control benefits.

Case of the Sarda-Yamuna Link

Following the Supreme Court's decision, some efforts were made to move the project along. However, it remained stunted. A case in point is the Sarda-Yamuna link project proposed by Atal Behari Vajpayee, when he was prime minister, 1999-2004. That project calls for linking of the Sarda river in Uttarakhand state (Uttaranchal in Figure 1) near its border with Nepal (see **Figure 3**) to the Yamuna River near Karnal in the state of Haryana, and from the Yamuna the canal water will be subsequently diverted to western parts of Rajasthan and Gujarat states. According to sources in the Irrigation Department, cited by the *Tribune of Punjab* in 2012, "the canal, having a capacity of 192 cubic meters per minute, will pass through Khatima, Sitarganj, and Kashipur, involving the Koshi and Ramganga rivers on its way. Small dams will be constructed on these rivers to facilitate the canal."

The project ran into difficulties when the state of Uttarakhand objected. According to Water Minister Bharti, in an interview with *India Today* published April 15, 2016, "what is happening is that no state is willing to accept that they have surplus water."

States with surplus water do not want their surplus water to be taken away, some states fearing that it could lead to future shortages in the state. So a proposed inter-basin water transfer needs a detailed study to ensure that the proposed transfer is sound. If a transfer is made without adequate investigation, the "done deal" could create future problems. It is for this reason that the in-

Dr. Rao's proposal was taken up in 1982 when the National Water Development Agency (NWDA) was set up to carry out pre-feasibility studies, and in 1999, a National Commission for Integrated Water Resources Development Plan (NCIWRDP) began reviewing the NWDA reports. In Oct. 2002, India's Supreme Court recommended that the government formulate a plan to link the major Indian rivers by the year 2012. The river linking project, in its full scope, involves building 30 links, 3,000 small and large reservoirs, and 12,500 km of canals to link 36 Himalayan and Peninsular rivers to effect 178 cubic kilometers of interbasin water transport annually. When completed,

FIGURE 2
Sarda-Yamuna Link

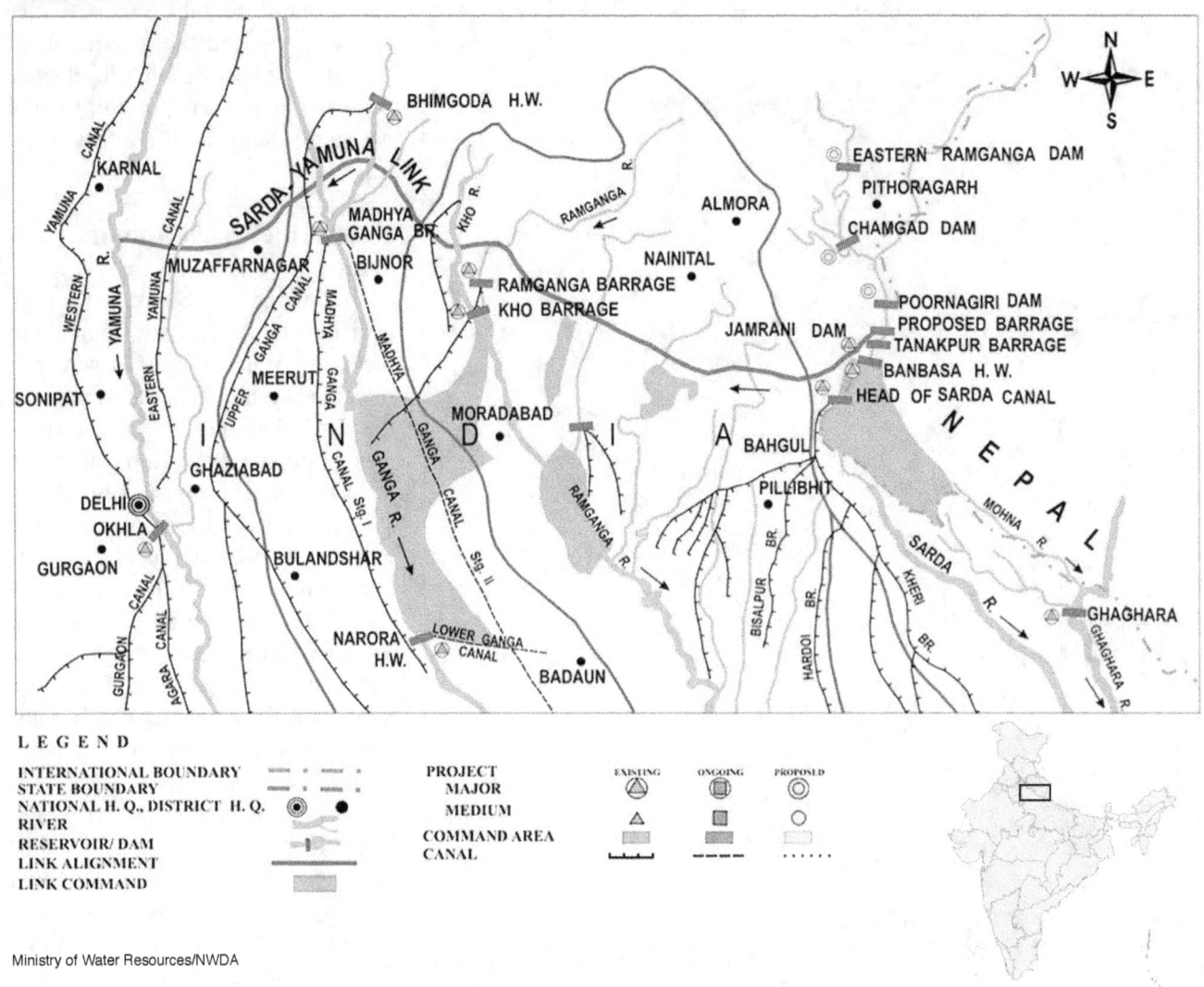

LEGEND

INTERNATIONAL BOUNDARY
STATE BOUNDARY
NATIONAL H. Q., DISTRICT H. Q.
RIVER
RESERVOIR/ DAM
LINK ALIGNMENT
LINK COMMAND

PROJECT
MAJOR
MEDIUM

COMMAND AREA
CANAL

EXISTING   ONGOING   PROPOSED

Ministry of Water Resources/NWDA

ter-basin transfer of water in the Murray-Darling river basin in Australia took almost 20 years. Referring to this uncertainty that creates fears over inter-basin transfers, Bharti said in her *India Today* interview that the Modi government is now planning detailed river basin studies. "We are doing a Memorandum of Understanding with the European Union and Australia, who have done similar work on the Danube and the Murray-Darling, the world's best river basin studies," she said.

Modi's Experience

Prime Minister Modi's commitment to the linking of India's rivers is clear. He made fast-tracking of the linking of rivers his top priority after becoming prime minister with a strong victory in the 2014 general elections. It is likely that Modi's conviction in this area stems from the benefit his state, Gujarat, derived at the time he was chief minister of the state, from the Sardar Sarovar Project—the western end of the Narmada River Basin Development Project—that contributed to the irrigation of 1.85 million hectares of land covering 3,112 villages and 15 districts of Gujarat state, in addition to helping to irrigate 246,000 hectares in desert districts in Rajasthan and 37,500 hectares in the hilly tract of Maharashtra state by pumping.

Modi is also keen to develop an Inland Water Transport Grid extending over 4,500 km on the lines of the National Highway grid. The *Times of India*, reporting on Aug. 9, 2014, just months after Modi became prime minister, said he had instructed the shipping ministry to develop these water routes for transportation of bulk cargo and bring them online as an alternative mode of transport. Cargo movement by such waterways is about 30% cheaper than by road, the article noted.

Construction and Obstruction

Modi is initially taking up those linking projects in which both rivers flow within the same state, in preference to the more contentious projects, which link rivers that flow through more than one state. An example is the Godavari and Krishna rivers, linked last September, and the proposed Ken-Betwa and Damanganga-Pinjal interlinking projects. Godavari and Krishna, the second and the fourth longest rivers in the country, were linked by a canal in the southern state of Andhra Pradesh. A second project, the Ken-Betwa link, is being constructed now in central India, primarily within the borders of Madhya Pradesh.[1] The Damanganga-Pinjal linking will take place entirely within the state of Maharashtra.

More challenging for Modi will be the linking of inter-state rivers. The Sutlej-Yamuna Canal is a case in point. Following the signing of the Indus Water Treaty between India and Pakistan in 1960, India was allocated the water rights for the rivers Sutlej, Beas, and Ravi from among those in the Indus river basin that traverse the India-Pakistan border. At the time, the water from these three rivers was shared among Punjab, Delhi, and Jammu and Kashmir. In 1966 the state of Haryana was carved out of Punjab. But the river Yamuna—that ran through undivided Punjab but now flowed only in Haryana and beyond it to the east—was never considered a part of this arrangement.

A water dispute emerged immediately between these two states, both highly dependent on agriculture. In 1976, then Prime Minister Indira Gandhi ruled that of the available 18.75 billion cubic meters of water from the three rivers, Punjab and Haryana would receive 4.3 billion each. Nothing, however, was resolved and construction of the canal was stopped in 1990.

In 2002, the Supreme Court issued a directive to the Punjab government to complete the canal. In 2004, however, the then state government of Punjab pushed through the state assembly the "Punjab Termination of Waters Agreement Act," which annulled all earlier accords and awards on the apportionment of river waters among the states of Punjab, Haryana, and Rajasthan. The half-finished canal remains in disrepair.

Addressing the Sarda-Yamuna link—the link proposed by former Prime Minister Vajpayee—which involves transferring waters from one state-based river to another river that runs through other states, Water Minister Bharti has cited the Pancheshwar Multipurpose Project (PMP) agreement that Prime Minister Modi signed with Nepal in 2014. She considers the PMP as the underpinning for developing the Sarda-Yamuna link, as she explained in a press briefing reported in *The Hindu* on Jan. 12, 2015. The PMP also concerns the Sarda River (known as the Mahakali in Nepal), which forms the international boundary between India and Nepal, and a bi-national storage-type hydropower project is to be developed on the river. It is scheduled to generate 6,720 megawatts of peak power and a live storage of 6.56 billion cubic meters of fresh water.

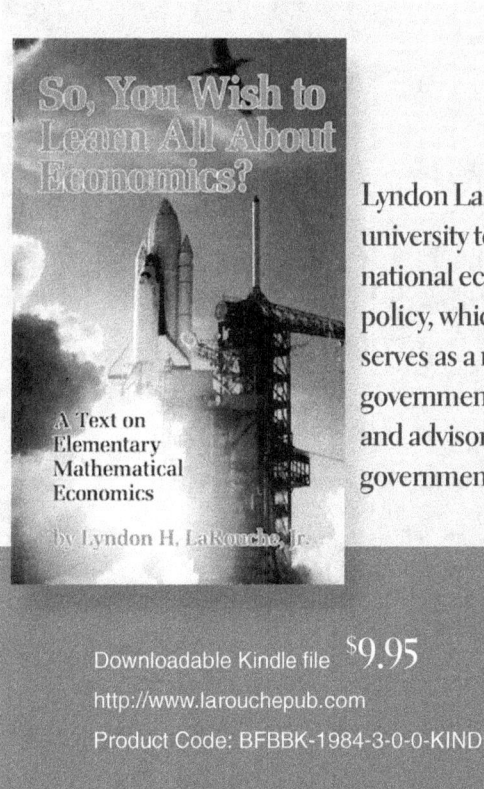

---

1. Ashok Swain, "Modi's Grand Plan to Divert Himalayan Rivers Faces Obstacles," *New Security Beat*, Wilson Center Environmental Change and Security Program, Dec. 22, 2015. https://www.newsecuritybeat.org/2015/12/modis-grand-plan-divert-himalayan-rivers-faces-obstacles/

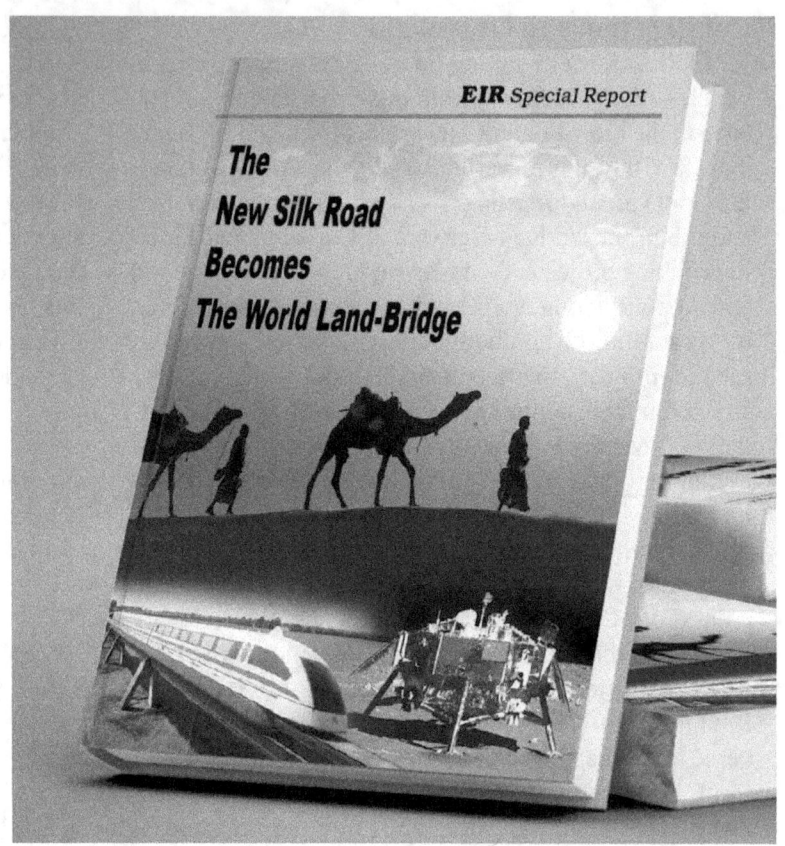

II. Revive the Space Program

Man in the Solar System and Beyond

Kesha Rogers addressed NASA veterans and others in Houston on May 14. This is an edited version of a transcript of her opening remarks there.

Okay, good afternoon, I'm Kesha Rogers, and I'm a member of the LaRouche PAC Policy Committee, and former candidate nominee for U.S. Congress. So, what we want to do today is to have this discussion in which I hope all of you have thought about some questions and ways to participate.

And this is the first step which we must take to look at the reason we're taking up the fight for understanding a completely new conception of what our space program has to represent. There's a lot that we still don't know, and we have yet to discover about the Universe in which we live, and the Solar system in which we live.

So what I want to do, just to start off the discussion, is to read a statement I just wrote:

LaRouche PAC

Kesha Rogers, shown here on an earlier LaRouche PAC webcast, addressed NASA veterans and others in Houston on May 14, emphasizing that "the commitment to space exploration must be based on the defense of the creative identity of the human mind."

The commitment to space exploration must be based on the defense of the creative identity of the human mind. Human beings are a space-faring species, not meant to be confined to Earth: a species with a mission to discover and come to understand who we are as mankind in the Universe. We must bring about a unified human mission that establishes a completely new view of the Solar system, defined not by the compartmentalization of space, but by a unified galactic system.

Visionary leaders like space pioneer Krafft Ehricke and President John F. Kennedy understood that the industrial development of the Moon and beyond is not just a worthwhile undertaking, but an extraterrestrial imperative. Today, China is leading the advance toward this extraterrestrial imperative with the steady progress of its lunar program.

For the last six years I have led a national campaign to defend our U.S. manned space program, which is fundamental to the progress of our nation's economic development, and provides the basis for peaceful relations among all nations. Our manned space program and the future of our nation have been under brutal attack since 2010, with the egregious cuts and dismantling of our space program, starting with Obama's cancellation of the Constellation program, and the cuts to the fusion science-driver program, important for the development of fusion propulsion technology, which is absolutely essential for the exploration of space. We must restore our commitment to a unified national mission dedicated to the exploration of space, starting with the development of the Moon (including its unique fusion resource, helium-3).

Where Are the Formulas?

This national mission will lay the basis for a much greater expansion of mankind throughout the Solar system, with Mars as the next target for human exploration and development. America needs a robust space exploration and development program to draw our nation's attention away from petty problems on Earth and to refocus attention once more on the excitement of exploration of the Universe, the thrill of discovery, and the conquest of new frontiers. This passion for adventure and yearning to stretch our horizon will surely drive the next generation of space explorers and inspire our nation for the next 100 years in space.

Rogers stated that Krafft Ehricke (1911-1984), a space expert and visionary leader, understood that space exploration is our extraterrestrial imperative.

What I would like to do is to attempt to draw on more of these conceptions throughout the course of this discussion today, and the questions and comments that you have will help us to develop those ideas further. But, let me just say that for the past several years that I've been leading this national fight in defense of the space program, one thing that's been very clear is that there's a very crucial aspect that has been missing from the equation. And this is the continued targeting of our space program by the enemies of progress,— and we'll talk a little bit more about Krafft Ehricke, and what Krafft Ehricke actually understood about the enemies of progress, as being really exemplified by the limits-to-growth Malthusian system, which asserts that there are limited resources on the planet Earth, and that there are limitations to man's understanding of the Universe in which we live. Krafft Ehricke had a completely different conception about that. And that's what has really been an underly-

President John F. Kennedy, another visionary leader, announced on May 25, 1961 before a special joint session of Congress, the goal of sending an American safely to the Moon before the end of that decade.

ing flaw and problem with the thinking amongst those mathematicians or the accounting figures that have taken over the control of the space program. They try to put limitations on mankind's progress.

Now, when you think about it, the human factor is the most essential factor in understanding what the mission of a unified space program has to be,— the factor of human creativity and the human mind. So, when you look at our campaign, don't just look at it from the standpoint of, "Oh, where are the technical aspects? Where are the formulas?" What is your formula to actually justify your understanding of man as a space-faring species? You're not going to find this formula. You have to find it within yourself, as a human being, with what must be a completely new conception of the identity of human beings on planet Earth, and throughout our Solar system, throughout the Universe and the Galaxy that we live in. And so, this conception of the creativity of the human mind, the human factor, is very critical. It's a principle to understand when you think about what the great pioneers of space exploration defined as our mission and purpose in the space program,— what is our extraterrestrial imperative?

And many times we have talked about the visionary role of Krafft Ehricke. I think he is extremely important to continue to go back to, because the conception of the playful, creative mind doesn't really exist in the domain of the society in which we live right now. You really want to think about how you imagine something that you have never known before, and how you create something which is totally new to the understanding of the human mind. And I'm going to go through that and expound on that, because that's going to be the basis of what I want you to take from my discussion today. I want to read again, Krafft Ehricke's conception of space travel. He says:

> The concept of space travel carries with it enormous impact, because it challenges man on practically all fronts of his physical and spiritual existence. The idea of traveling to other celestial bodies reflects to the highest degree the independence and agility of the human mind. It lends ultimate dignity to man's technical and scientific endeavors. Above all, it touches on the philosophy of his very existence.

And that's something to think about, because the problem is that we have been denied access to understanding what is the real philosophy of the existence of man. And this has been an ongoing fight since the development of mankind, that the existence of man is something which in many eyes is disconnected from, and has no relationship to the Universe in which we live.

So this is something that for the past several decades, Mr. LaRouche has taken up as a critical principle in understanding the exploration of a true mission for space conquest. That is not just something that you do because you have a bunch of money, and you want to go build tourist attractions on the Moon, and you want to turn space travel into Wall Street profiteering: get up there cheap, get up there quick. But unless you talk about the ability of the human mind, the nature of creating a culture in society that fosters human creativity,— then what you're doing with the space program is just a fraud.

What We Don't Know

This is completely essential to what Mr. LaRouche's program for the space program has been, as a continuation of what President John F. Kennedy had set into motion. President John F. Kennedy knew that the development of space, development of new frontiers in technological discoveries,— as did Krafft Ehricke, as did the great pioneers before him, Wernher von Braun, Oberth, Goddard, these pioneers, and rocket scientists,— knew that we have an imperative to conquer the Solar system,

John F. Kennedy Library

Kesha Rogers said that Lyndon LaRouche's space program has been a continuation of what President John Kennedy set into motion. Here, Kennedy is inspecting the interior of Friendship 7, the capsule via which John Glenn (to the right of Kennedy) became the first American to orbit Earth.

so that we can actually bring about a new conception of the unified development of mankind as a whole.

And in a paper written in 1986, I believe it was, Mr. LaRouche talks about a very important concept called "Spiritual Imperative for the Conquest of Space," and I think this really gets at the spark which has to be understood.

Now before I read this quote, I want you to think about this from the standpoint that there are technological and other things that have to be developed, in terms of developing space. When you talk about what's necessary for the colonization of the Moon, for building colonies on the Moon, for the exploration of Mars,— Do we just go up there? Is it just, "OK, we just got there." I said this before, I take people who come into Houston, sometimes, and they're mesmerized by the Saturn V rocket. And if you go to visit the Saturn V rocket, you see this masterpiece, and this giant rocket,— it's being preserved, sitting in this warehouse, that everyone from all over the world comes to see. Something that, when this was developed, nations throughout the world were participating in. But more so, they were gaining the benefits of what the Saturn V rocket—as a continuation of that program—was to represent.

But my point is that if you look at this great masterpiece, you can't just say, "Oh, this was just thrown together." This was an engineering feat. What was the skilled labor, the engineering, every single facet of econ-

EIRNS/Stuart Lewis

Lyndon LaRouche wrote of the "Spiritual Imperative for the Conquest of Space." As a result of the unique creativity of mankind, discoveries are made that enable man to go into space, and which benefit the entire world. Here LaRouche addresses a conference in Sterling, Va. in 2013 on the implications of space science for a new paradigm for mankind.

omy, that went into the building of this work? And even more, what was the human factor that went into it? The human factor also of people who dedicated their lives to the establishment of this great project which took men to the Moon. And that was almost a mission that did not happen, because lives were lost. And as we experienced in the battlefields of war, and when people commit themselves to a fight in military warfare,— they know that they're going in with the understanding that they may not come out. Their lives may not exist any longer. But the commitment always has to be to the betterment and the progress of mankind, *coming from your society as a whole*.

And that's the difference from the conception that we see today, with the policy toward our space program that is murderous, that does not take human life truly into account. When you want to put Wall Street, and the financial private institutions at the forefront of the development of our space program, and they say, "Oh, I'll give you a few pennies, if we have something left over." Every single thing, every single penny, has to go into the development of space exploration based on the idea that the human mind and the human life has to be protected and preserved.

What LaRouche says makes the point clear: "Human beings are absolutely distinguished from the beasts by virtue of the fact that every newborn infant has 'the divine spark of reason.' This spark, if developed, enables each of us to develop the power of creative rea-

soning, the quality of reasoning typified by the work of the best scientific discoverers."

He goes on to say, "One new, useful idea, discovered by such an individual mind is a benefit for all mankind."

And it's very similar to the idea that when mankind goes out into space, when you have an astronaut go out and orbit the Earth, when we go to the Moon,— this isn't just something that the astronaut is doing to go on a joy ride. He is actually doing this because the entire nation is going with him to participate in this. The entire world is benefitting from this discovery, as all of the world benefits from a great scientific discovery, such as a discovery of Einstein, or a musical discovery of a great Classical composer.

And that's the culture which we have to re-instill in our society, and that's the culture which has right now been eliminated by the lack of a space program policy under President Obama, who is putting trillions of dollars into upgrading the nuclear arsenal, and putting missile defense weapons on the borders of China and Russia,— instead of actually calling for collaboration with these nations, based on the idea that mankind has to commit itself to a new paradigm based on cooperation among nations. I thought it was very fitting, that just recently, the cosmonauts from the International Space Station sent the message down on the 71st anniversary of the defeat of fascism, defeat of the Nazis in Germany, saying that peaceful relations, cooperation, and scientific development among nations is only going to be possible in a world without war.

A world without war starts with understanding what we have to commit ourselves to from the standpoint of a new paradigm based on the cooperation among nations for shared achievements, for the advancement of man's mastery over new fundamental principles, and for the implementation of new forms of technology.

That really gets to the conception of why we're looking, with great excitement and vigor, at what China is doing with its space program. But you have China doing something that no other nation has yet embarked on: Venturing out to discover, based on the idea that it is our imperative to go to and master what is out there on the far side of the Moon. Now we're not necessarily going, already knowing what's there. We have some ideas, but that's the beauty of the discoveries of mankind, you're not going and saying, "Oh, okay, this is what we're going to look for, and this is what we want

Tim Pearce

Saturn V was a masterpiece in which nations throughout the world participated, and also benefited from the continuation of that program.

to find." It takes away a sense of creativity if you're already thinking, "Oh, we're already there. We've already mastered everything." And that's what is so unique about what China is doing, and China really continues to follow what we exemplified in the past under leadership such as that of President John F. Kennedy. Everybody remembers John F. Kennedy's Moon speech, but it had this principle: "We're going to do something that we don't know." We went to the Moon. When we stepped foot on the Moon, we didn't know what was going to happen. We didn't know what we were going to find, but we knew that it was our imperative, our prerogative, to embark on this mission. And I was reading about how the people within mission control, like Gene Kranz, were saying, "I don't know about this President, but he really believed in us, and he believed in this nation, and I thought that this was too far out there. But I saw that we had a President that had vision, and who said, 'where there is no vision the people will perish.'" That was the idea that Kennedy had committed to the people.

Why Bach?

So that's the idea, and that's the conception right now, that you're getting from nations like Russia and China, nations that want to have mankind embark on a new frontier of cooperation and collaboration in which we can participate if we have the right leadership. It's very fitting that while,— On the one hand you have a drive for war and economic collapse coming from the United States, and coming from under the directives of President Obama, and those Wall Street operations that he submits to. You think about the difference in that drive toward war, which actually creates more suicides, as we're seeing, more killing in the society which has been completely devastated, but, on the other hand you look at the optimism that you're seeing coming from what Russian President Vladimir Putin just did—which was a beautiful indication of his commitment to the progress of mankind—when just recently, the Russians held a concert in Palmyra, in the ruins of Palmyra, in what was an ancient amphitheater in Syria, just after—just a few months ago, this area was just used for brutal warfare, and killing of human beings. And President Putin of Russia called for a concert.

And I'd just like to just say this, just think about this. This concert, as was reported in a recent article, did not begin with a piece by a Russian composer. Instead, the Russians chose to begin with a potent piece by Johann Sebastian Bach, the famous *Chaconne,* Partita for Solo Violin No. 2 in B minor. The writer says that the great violinist Yehudi Menuhin called the *Chaconne* "the greatest structure for solo violin that exists," and violinist Joshua Bell has said, "the *Chaconne* is not just one of the greatest pieces of music ever written, but one of the greatest achievements of any man in history. It's a spiritually powerful piece, emotionally powerful, and structurally perfect."

If you disconnect these things, you will say, "OK, that's nice, but why did you bring that up?" Well, I bring that up because there has to be a connection between space exploration and a culture that fosters human creativity, Classical culture, the culture of the human mind. If you go back and look at the role of the great pioneers, such as Krafft Ehricke, they brought with them the greatest of Western culture and Classical culture, as an expression of what our space program has to be. You can't have a space program with Beyoncé and Jay Z, and so forth. You have to have a space program that exemplifies a true commitment to the human creative identity.

Every Day Counts In Today's Showdown To Save Civilization

III. The FBI Can't Stop Lyndon LaRouche

9/11 Today

by Tony Papert

How should you deal with the experience which some had on 9/11 or immediately after, Lyndon LaRouche asked during an internal discussion on May 22. It must be presented systematically. To begin with, the people of Manhattan must be put through the terror of Sept. 11, 2001, step by step (although not howl by howl or scream by scream). They must get the full blast of the cruelty and evil plainly and clearly, as it was carried out by means of the Saudis, with the complicity of the FBI, on behalf of the British Royals. Lyndon LaRouche was watching it unfold live on television, while he was simultaneously being interviewed on the radio. He saw each of the two planes from Boston, with its passengers made prisoners and sent to their deaths into the Twin Towers by the Saudis, along with many other innocent people who were in the buildings. Mass deaths. It is essential to put out the plain facts; don't let the FBI get away with its lying. The impact of this issue, the fact that that happened, is what must be considered. This was a mass murder by the Saudis. You have to convict the evil ones on the basis of these deeds,— including the British Queen. You have to clean the deck of these crimes, by satisfying the demands for justice of the people of New York and elsewhere.

Michael Steger, the LaRouche PAC Policy Committee leader of San Francisco, then spoke to the effect that indeed the 28 secret pages of the report of the Joint Congressional Inquiry into 9/11, on the Saudi role, must be released, as demanded by H. Res. 14; and the Justice Against Sponsors of Terrorism Act (JASTA), which will allow 9/11 families to sue Saudi Arabia, and which passed the U.S. Senate on May 17, must be enacted. But while we support these mea-sures, our concerns and our goals are much broader; we must approach this from a much higher level, he said.

The intent of the 9/11 attacks was for a coup and dictatorship by Bush and Cheney,— which nearly succeeded. The intent was to enable the series of regime-change wars launched by Bush-Cheney and Obama, from Afghanistan to Iraq, Libya, and Syria, all building up to a thermonuclear showdown with Russia and China, which will offer them the choice of total surrender, or, if they refuse, thermonuclear destruction of human civilization or even the human species itself.

Now we have to reverse this, and restore Constitutional government to the United States in collaboration with Russia and China, as Franklin Roosevelt intended. That must be the intent of the U.S. Presidency today; that embodies our higher standpoint.

Lyndon LaRouche responded, "Exactly that. Yes, exactly that. We are human beings. We have lives of limited duration, but we also have the potential of understanding the processes to which we are subjected. Experience as a subjective matter is something that human beings can and must understand. Once they have understood the problem and its implications ... It's like the guy going in for a surgical operation, and he thinks he is not going to live through the surgery. But then he finds out that he is able to survive. And suddenly he has a different attitude about life, once he grabs that idea. Our job is to encourage people to take a justified understanding of this kind of experience. Because by understanding what this is all about, and the effect of that on the people, you are freeing the people of the threat which otherwise harbors around them."

Dissolve NATO and Create A New Westphalian System

Europe must follow Putin's lead to stop pre-emptive thermonuclear war!

by Michael Steger

*May 21—In 1973 the secret po-
lice-state apparatus often known
as the Federal Bureau of Imbe-
ciles, or FBI, targeted leading international political activist and
economist Lyndon H. LaRouche,
Jr. for elimination by the FBI-con-
trolled Communist Party USA.
This is the same FBI which was
created by the British Empire in
the early Twentieth Century to
eliminate German and Renaissance culture from the United
States, and which was deployed in
1944-1945 to destroy Franklin
Delano Roosevelt's legacy and the
memory of his leadership. It was
the same FBI which then played a
hand in the 9/11 terrorist attacks
that killed 3,000 Americans, and
the same FBI which today continues the cover-up of its
intended and nearly successful fascist coup on 9/11.*

*At the May 9 Victory Day Parade in Moscow, celebrating the 71st anniversary of the
defeat of Nazi Germany, Putin declared that Russia wanted to create a modern
nonaligned system of international security with all states.*

If the United States and the trans-Atlantic world are
to escape this cycle of self-destruction and the satanic
influence of the FBI—whose source is the very heart of
the British Empire—then the entire Cold War system,
that is, the IMF-Wall Street-London financial and
NATO security system, established by the British
Crown and its U.S. lackeys such as the Dulles brothers
and Hoover's FBI—must be dissolved, and in the
coming weeks. Germany has a key role to play, as does
Japan. As Japan now moves closer to Russia, and im-
plicitly China, and distances itself from the implosion
of the trans-Atlantic system, Germany must take the
critical step and reassert German and European inter-

ests in collaboration with Russia, ending every excuse
for the nuclear build-up now threatening nuclear anni-
hilation.

This opportunity is greatly strengthened as a result
of the brilliant flanking actions and initiatives under-
taken by Russian President Vladimir Putin in recent
weeks. In his speech delivered at the May 9 Moscow
Victory Day Parade, which was observing the 71st anniversary of the defeat of Nazi Germany, he issued a
call for all nations to join a "non-aligned" security
system against terrorism. He said:

> History lessons teach us that peace on Earth is
> not established by itself; that one needs to be
> cautious; that double standards as well as short-
> sighted indulgence of those who nurture crimi-

nal plans are impermissible ... Today, civilization is again facing cruelty and violence: terrorism has become a global threat. We must defeat this evil; Russia is open to joining efforts with all states and is ready to work on creating a modern, non-aligned system of international security.

Since the direct intervention into Syria by Russian forces in late September 2015, the actions of Putin's Russia, combined with the collaborative steps taken by China, now threaten to end the entire post-9/11 hyper- accelerated drive for global fascism and population reduction, a drive which has been imposed on the world by British assets since the removal of Bismarck as German Chancellor in 1890 and the assassination of President McKinley in 1901.

German Foreign Minister Frank-Walter Steinmeier emphasized May 18 the close connection between politics and economic collaboration, underlining the importance of German economic collaboration with Russia and China. He said the train route from China to Germany symbolized a common security partnership from Vancouver to Vladivostok.

There is a specific current in Germany which wants to return to its better traditions of the post-war period. If Germany breaks now from British-NATO control, other European countries will follow, and the danger of nuclear war will be significantly reduced. Turkey, Ukraine, Georgia, and the Balkan nations will no longer be nuclear pawns in a British geopolitical game. And Europe may finally reverse the devastation of U.S.-British sponsored warfare along the entire southern and eastern coast of the Mediterranean with economic reconstruction.

As German Foreign Minister Frank-Walter Steinmeier said in Berlin at a May 18 Business Conference of the Organization for Security and Co-operation in Europe (OSCE), "... Most of all because we want to talk about political visions, and this in times of grave political turmoil. It is an experiment, because we want to talk about concrete cooperation, and this in times in which violent conflicts in our common area demand an almost daily toll of human lives. It is an experiment because we want to talk about economic practice, and this in times when many believe that our visions for a common area of security and stability have been cut into pieces."

Referring to the China-to-Germany rail line, he said, "this amazing route across several climatic zones

shows which geographical challenges are connected with the intent to shape our common area, a common area which spans from our trans-Atlantic partners via Europe to Asia."

He went on to say, "At the same time, I see in this route the great economic dynamic that is unfolding already in this area or can still unfold its potential. And, the visit of the Chinese President to Duisburg [Germany] shows how important it is that politics deals with questions of the economy, and vice versa." This train route symbolizes the "importance of the vision of a common security partnership from Vancouver to Vladivostok. And that, ladies and gentlemen, is a vision to which we must commit ourselves."

As for the United States, we have now committed the greatest acts of destruction in the modern age, in just over the last 15 years since 9/11. We threaten the world with nuclear war, both in Eastern Europe and the South China Sea. We have spread terrorism, drugs, and a culture of death from Afghanistan to Algeria. And the population in the United States suffers increasingly from drug abuse, suicide, despair, mass unemployment, and outrage.

As is now clear, the British Empire no longer rules the world, it only destroys it. Everything under its control faces an accelerated demise which threatens uncontrolled nuclear war, best indicated by the behavior of the United States under Bush and Obama. It is now Russia and China, under the leadership of Vladimir Putin, which have asserted the existence of a higher domain, one of actual victory, not won by killing, but by means of a system for long-term human survival. In other words, a new Westphalian system from Vladivostok to Vancouver, Beijing to San Francisco, increasingly rules the world.

And so it must, if we are to survive.

Germany's Choice

Germany is currently sending troops—a deployment probably of battalion size—to the border of Russia, a step not taken since the Nazis' Operation Bar-

China Daily

German Foreign Minister Steinmeier said on May 18 that the 2014 visit by Chinese President Xi Jinping (second from right) to Duisburg, Germany, a terminal for the Land-bridge railway from China, demonstrated the closeness of politics and economics. Duisburg is the world's largest inland port.

barossa blitzkrieg attempt of World War II. This coincides with the Obama-British plan for further military provocations against Russia, as already seen in the Ukraine coup orchestrated by Victoria Nuland and her NATO-sponsored Nazis in 2013, otherwise known as Victoria's Secret. Add to this the inauguration of missile defense systems in Romania and Poland, celebrated this past week, which counter Russia's defensive second-strike capabilities,— and the threat of a pre-emptive nuclear strike by NATO has never been greater. From Russia's standpoint, with NATO under British and Obama direction, war again is in prospect, and this time it will entail nuclear attack.

Couple this with the Weimar-style hyperinflation of negative interest rates in Japan, Denmark, Sweden, Switzerland, and Norway, and the massive money-printing program of Mario Draghi's European Central Bank, now 80 billion Euro per month,— and Germany seems once again to have been suckered into acting as the British puppet for war against Russia.

Germany must act, and within the coming weeks, to end the sanctions regime against Russia. Germany must again lead the other nations of Europe, and it can, but only by engaging in the foreign policy tradition of Bismarck, who insisted on collaboration with both France and Russia, and by looking eastward towards the development of Eurasia. Nations such as France, Italy, Austria, Greece, Hungary, and the Czech Republic have each disavowed, in different ways, the sanctions regime against Russia as detrimental to economic growth and international security. The sanctions are the very basis for NATO military escalation, and their removal will enable European integration into the vibrant development program of the "One Belt One Road" policy now dominating Eurasia.

Squirrels Invade Washington

The United States today is British-occupied territory, just as Vichy France was occupied by the British-sponsored Nazis during World War II. As was true then, the media hails the occupation as a success. The corruption since 9/11, under both Bush and Obama, has promoted a program of fascism domestically and has targeted the nations of Russia and China for submission to aggression, according to the program of the British Empire's leading geopolitician Halford Mackinder of eliminating any threat from Eurasia. The bloody act of 9/11 itself, run by the British and the Saudis with accomplices inside the United States' rogue security apparatus, was nothing less than a fascist coup attempt, and the U.S. political class and media are guilty accomplices in war crimes committed over these last fifteen years.

The outrage that now dominates American politics is the direct result of capitulation by the leadership of both parties to the fascist program of Bush and Obama. The cowardice of Nancy Pelosi and the Democratic Party leadership in failing to impeach Dick Cheney and George W. Bush, actually pales in comparison with the explicit protection that Republicans such as John Boehner and Paul Ryan have given to Obama and his perpetuation of his heinous crimes, such as his Terror Tuesdays. The entire political establishment in the United States is now facing chaos. Hillary Clinton as a human being has been destroyed by Obama. Bernie Sanders' campaign is a British-run chaos operation. The political parties are destroyed, and the rise of Trump's populist fascism, which bears a striking resemblance to that of Vichy's favorite fascist, Jacques Doriot, is a direct result of Obama's further destruction of the United States.

Thus, we are witnesses to the destruction of the British Empire in its entirety, not dissimilar to what was witnessed in the fall of the Roman Empire. The means to prevent this threat of massive population destruction, as we saw in the dark ages of Europe, is the immediate impeachment of Obama and the end of the Wall Street-NATO system of war and death, and its replacement by

Lithuania Ministry of National Defense

Countering Russian and Chinese efforts to develop economic collaboration to ensure long-term human survival, the Obama-British plan seeks provocations against Russia and China. Here, a rotating U.S. military company with its weapons and vehicles is deployed in Lithuania for training. The same maneuvers have taken place in other Baltic nations and Poland.

the New Westphalian System now developing in Asia, led by Putin.

For those gullible enough to fall for Trump, such as Alex Jones, Wayne Madsen, and Louis Farrakhan,— only to name a few among the many disgruntled suckers of America,— they may be surprised to find themselves, under Trump, perhaps at one of his holy casinos, somehow tied naked to a wooden post while Trump himself parades in a tiger costume hungry for future conquests. Rather fitting for the collapse of the Roman Empire. But those who study history would find such an image appropriate for the myriad prostitutes of popularity that are so common in the ongoing collapse of the British Empire's trans-Atlantic system today.

True leadership against fascism is something else.

LaRouche and Putin

In terms of historical comparisons, one might draw the conclusion that Lyndon LaRouche is similar to Charles de Gaulle. As had de Gaulle, so has LaRouche opposed the fascist occupation of his nation, almost as one lone individual, providing a living sense of the true United States last seen under the Presidency of Franklin Roosevelt. Given the role that Roosevelt played in defining victory in World War II,— as when he told an angry Winston Churchill that we are not fighting a war to defeat fascism simply to restore the British Empire's system of slavery,— one might draw the conclusion that Vladimir Putin, with his profound intervention with the Prayer for Palmyra concert, as in his intervention into the Syrian war against ISIS, and more broadly in his leadership against the ongoing threat of nuclear world war,— performs today the role of Franklin Roosevelt.

Although this comparison may be useful as a mnemonic device for the American layman today, it falls far short of disclosing the gravity of the global strategic setting within which we find ourselves, and the unique role that Lyndon LaRouche has played in reviving a global leadership to end the British Empire, once and for all. *Britannia delenda est!*

Putin's efforts since the Second Chechen War, in tandem with LaRouche's intervention with his 1999 "Storm Over Asia" analysis,— a presentation of the British intent for full conquest of Russia and China before the trans-Atlantic financial system should hemorrhage and die,— has been the critical foundation for ending the Bush-Cheney-Obama coup in the United States and freeing Europe from the British-imposed bureaucracy of the European Union and NATO's fascist war agenda.

Patriots of the United States must rally to the work and efforts of LaRouche, for no other figure combines the greatest tradition of the United States with such a well defined and demonstrated conception of mankind's future potential as a creative species. As Putin and his collaborators in China—such as President Xi Jinping—work to end the threat of nuclear war through the most comprehensive development of humanity that has ever been initiated in history, the action to break the British Empire's destruction of the trans-Atlantic region now depends on a higher courage, one to act for the greater good of mankind and independent from the cynicism and despair on which fascism feeds. We must now embark upon a Renaissance.

And this Renaissance depends on the actions of Putin, China, Germany, and the leadership of LaRouche in the United States. Nothing less will suffice, anything else will fail.

LaRouche's Triple Curve

Great endeavors in human history have been lost for the sake of a pseudo-religious belief in what are considered by popular opinion to be the necessary prerequisite steps for victory. Moses himself encountered such corruption as he led his people through the desert some 3,000 years ago. Although such prerequisites are often identified—in the hindsight of a successful outcome—as necessary steps, only the foolishness of a mathematician would make possible the belief that such formulae resemble anything like the basis for actually accomplishing a fundamental transformation in the historical trajectory of human development.

It is a unique accomplishment within trans-Atlantic society and over the last 50 years of cultural degeneration, that Lyndon La-Rouche has rejected any tendency toward, and overcome all influences of, reductionist thought in his strategic intervention, and for this reason, the FBI has failed to eliminate his international influence. But it has been successful in corrupting much of his organization, although the leading participants in La-Rouche's movement could not deny that they had been warned of such corrosive intellectual tendencies. His unjust imprisonment in 1989 at the hands of George H.W. Bush and his British Crown control-

lers left his organization susceptible to the insidious conceptions of Bertrand Russell and his opportunistic sycophants that LaRouche had clearly rejected as his first step towards achieving the foundation of a higher economic and strategic program of human development.

Above all, LaRouche's intent was not simply a new economic system, which we finally see manifest in the Eurasian System—also referred to as the BRICS, based largely on the collaboration of Russia, China, and India—but the scientific recognition of the higher domain of human creative thought and its willful development through the power of creative imagination, based upon the classical compositional principles of especially Bach, Mozart, Beethoven.

The Collapse Reaches a Critical Point of Instability

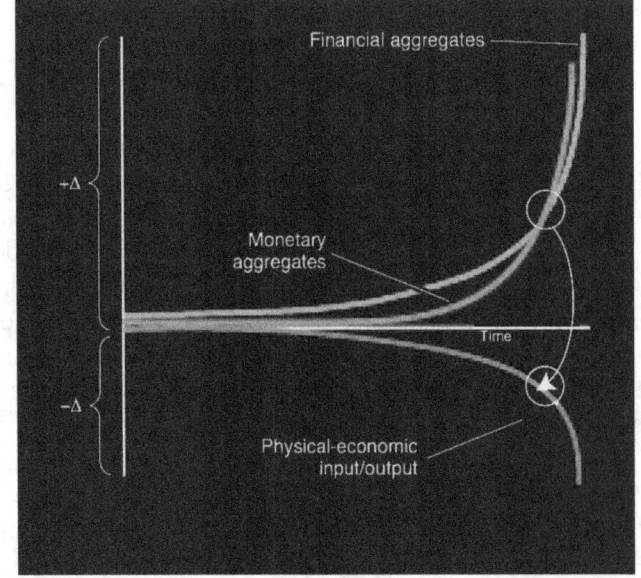

EIR, Jan.25, 2002

The Folly

It was this higher ordering principle of thought which was manifest in 1995 when LaRouche defined the Triple Curve function of economic collapse. In presenting the concept at a conference of associates in February 1996, he opened his presentation with remarks such as these:

"What is dooming us is our people; what our people believe. Because these people we like to blame,— we talk about the 'crooked politicians,' we talk about the conspirators on Wall Street, we talk about this, we talk about that, always blaming someone else. And if they're a public figure, as in the old days, when some people wore top hats, it was more fun to throw a snowball at a top hat. So we always blame somebody else. Now, the job of a leader is not to blame leaders. We can point out some are bad, some are defective, some are utterly immoral, some are barely human. But the problem lies in the people, not in the leaders. The problem, often, of oppression, lies in the oppressed. Because they will not accept any proposition that is not consistent with the assumption that they must remain 'the oppressed.'"

It may be that LaRouche's driving intention behind the Triple Curve function was to make clear that the tragedy befalling our nation and civilization itself, is not simply found in the relationships among the accelerating increase of financial instruments, the even greater increase in the acceleration of the monetary supply, and the accelerating collapse of real physical production—although they are important. It is that our very conception of our human identity in the universe has become fatally flawed, perhaps not irretrievably so, but recoverable only with serious repentance for the grave systemic errors of society which are so often nobly cloaked in the justifications of popularity, statistical probability, or the Hamlet syndrome, by which ungodly steps are taken merely to fight another day, a day—or a fight—which never seems to come.

Perhaps the greatest proof of such evil corruption of our society is seen in LaRouche's own unjust imprisonment. For only by putting the leading economist and political figure in the United States behind bars, were then the economic compromises, made in the wake of the Fall of the Berlin Wall that LaRouche had uniquely forecast six years earlier, even feasible—economic folly so accurately captured in the Triple Curve function.

It is now time to learn the lessons of the past, to join with Lyndon LaRouche in the most ennobling mission in mankind's history, and find success in doing what is considered by most to be the impossible, which is actually the practical, since it is in that mission, and only in that mission, that success is ever to be found.

www.ingramcontent.com/pod-product-compliance
Lightning Source LLC
Chambersburg PA
CBHW081203280526
45787CB00008B/3387